MW01180711

Gifts for a
Joyous
Christmas

from the Kids
at Boys Town

Gifts for a Joyous Christmas

from the Kids at Boys Town

Val J. Peter

BOYS TOWN, NEBRASKA

Gifts for a Joyous Christmas

Published by the Boys Town Press
Father Flanagan's Boys' Home
Boys Town, Nebraska 68010
www.girlsandboystown.org

© 2000 Father Flanagan's Boys' Home

All rights reserved. No part of this book may
be reproduced or transmitted in any form or by
any means, electronic or mechanical, including
photocopying, recording, or by any information
storage and retrieval system, without the written
permission of Boys Town, except where permitted
by law. For information, address Boys Town Press,
Father Flanagan's Boys' Home, 14100 Crawford St.,
Boys Town, NE 68010.

ISBN 1-889322-39-3

The Boys Town Press is the publishing
division of Girls and Boys Town, the
original Father Flanagan's Boys' Home.

Table of Contents

NOTE: *Boys Town is a family, and like every family, we cherish our children's privacy. In this book, our children share their thoughts with you, but their names have been changed to protect their privacy.*

CHAPTER 1

Catch the Christmas Spirit

There are two steps you need to take to get in the Christmas spirit. They are simple and straightforward. And they work.

The first step is to "right your relationship" with yourself, others, and God. You don't have to do it all in one day, but today is a good day to start.

On this first day you have to tell
yourself you're not going to be so
grumpy. So you have to be less
grumpy inside yourself. And you have
to let the good Lord give you a big
hug. That's right: You have to put
away your sadness and let the good
Lord give you a big hug.

The second step is to turn to
children and listen to them.

Through the years we have had
wonderful kids at Boys Town who
have learned the lesson of how to get
the Christmas spirit. Listen to the
memories that some of our alumni
have of Christmas here. Let them
touch your heart.

A. J.'s Christmas of 1927

I remember especially the Christmas of 1927 when I was eight years old. We had a lot of fun together. My children later in life asked me why I did not get discouraged or complain or fall into self-pity since I had no family at Christmas.

The answer is to be found in the faith that was passed on to me there at Boys Town. I mean this. Jesus had nothing at Christmas when He was born and He was Lord of everything. So, I knew I should not complain. The Mass meant more to me than I can possibly say.

Mike's Christmas of 1957

My thoughts go back to that first Christmas I spent at Boys Town. I noticed some of my classmates did not receive any gifts from back home. It was then I came to realize that some of them had no one else or at least no one who could afford to send them a Christmas present.

This realization was the greatest gift I received that Christmas of 1957. It relieved me of my self-pity. It brought me to the realization that the world is full of less fortunate people. I am truly a better person today because I learned gratitude the Christmas of 1957.

Louie's Christmas of 1968

I was only 11 years old. I came to Boys Town because I was an orphan. I had no father and my mother took ill with tuberculosis and died very young. We had no other family members who had any room for us. We were four brothers and no home to live in.

I remember that first Christmas at Boys Town. No presents for me? My heart was broken. Some kids received many gifts from home and some just one from home, but one was more than I had. When they finished distributing the gifts from home, someone said, "Who still doesn't have a present?" I was embarrassed, but I raised my hand anyway. They walked up to me. They gave me a big hug and a present and said, "Merry Christmas."

This may seem strange, but I remember that little bit of sharing and how it changed my whole life.

On Christmas Day, I took a walk by myself down by the lake near the grade school. The first thing I did was thank God – deep down in my heart. I thought no one would care enough to give me a present. I was wrong. And by the way, guess what? I took St. Nicholas as my confirmation name.

CHAPTER 2

Reflections

I like to tell the story of St. Jerome, who was praying at the Christmas manger at Bethlehem. He said, "Lord Jesus, I give you all my work." The Lord said, "Thank you, Jerome, but don't you have something more to give me?" Jerome said, "Lord, I give you my prestige and my honor."

The Lord said, "Jerome, don't you have something more to give me?" Jerome said, "I give you my health and all the good things that I have." And the Lord said, "Jerome, don't you have something more to give me?" Jerome said, "I don't have anything more important to give you." Jesus said, "Yes, you do, Jerome. I want to take away your sins and bring you joy."

In this Christmas season, this is what the Lord wants from us:

- our sins
- our troubles
- our anger
- our resentment
- our envy

- our cussedness
- our inability to say "I love you"
- our inability to receive gifts and joy

In other words, the Lord wants to fill our lives with gratitude.

Happy Holidays!

CHAPTER 3

Christmas Dinner

Children have wonderful ideas about how to make a holiday celebration special. Here's how our Wegner Middle School students would create a festive holiday meal.

If I could serve Christmas dinner, I think people would like it. I would not only serve food and drinks, but intangible things like loving, caring, giving, forgiveness, thankfulness, and familiness.

Christmas is a time to reflect on the birth of Jesus Christ. You should think about what Jesus sacrificed for us so we could live forever.

At dinner, I would probably bring out the Bible and read about the birth of Jesus. I would serve mashed potatoes, pie, rice, corn, turkey, ham, stuffing, and pudding. I would spend a lot of time making the food. That is another way to show love.

— KIM

I would serve a 50-foot Christmas cookie in the form of a tree.

— STEVEN

I would serve a turkey dinner with vanilla milk shakes. I also would serve a chamomile tea. Along with my grand dinner, I would serve up a plate of love, a cup of kindness, and a gallon of hope. I would also pass out little gifts. They would have rings inside that said, "Merry Christmas to all."

— MARTIN

If I were to cook Christmas dinner, I would first sit down and think of what to cook. Ah! I have it. A nice big turkey and feast. But it probably wouldn't work out. The turkey would get burned, the stuffing would be almost liquid, the pickles would be sour, the bread would be moldy, the jam would be gone, and we wouldn't have eggnog. Darn it! Now, I've got to think of another solution. I might be able to go to the store, but no, the store is closed. I have it! Why don't I take everybody to eat out? I have enough cash. But where? Of course! How about a nice seafood dinner at Red Lobster? That would be perfect! It is convenient, and it's also a treat.

— MATT

For Christmas dinner I would like to serve some of my mother's good finger-licking chicken with a drop of hot sauce to add a kick.

I would also like to serve some of my favorite stuffing that my mom makes, and add a cup of hot chili peppers. For drinks, I will have a lot of water and some punch.

For dessert, I will have some apple pie, banana cream pie, and some pumpkin pie. My dinner will make everybody's day more enjoyable.

— JERRY

For Christmas dinner I would try to cook a turkey for the main meal, and stuffing to go with it. One thing I wouldn't make is liver, because it doesn't go with it. I would also make some spiced meat and some salsa on the side. For a tasty dessert, I would make apple pie, cherry pie, and a pumpkin pie.

— ARIANA

What I will serve for Christmas dinner is both love and food. First of all, the best thing of all is sweet love, delicious hugs, genuine kisses, finger-licking conversations, breathtaking fun. Then another thing I will serve is outrageous laughing, cheerful crying, happiness, joy, playing, and singing. The next thing I will serve is finger-licking greens, glazed straight out-of-the-oven ham, roasted turkey, delicious stuffing, sweet cranberries, delicious double fudge chocolate cake, and sweet golden glistening hot cornbread. These are the things that will be served on Christmas. Love and food will be the only things served under my roof.

— TREONE

I would serve turkey, ham, yams with marshmallows, ice cream, cookies, cakes, mashed potatoes, carrots, peas, pies, bread and gravy, bread sticks, juice, deviled eggs. Another thing that I'd serve: 1 cup of love, 1 cup of hugs, 1 cup of kisses, 5 cups of family. That's what I'd serve for Christmas dinner.

— MICKEY

I would serve macaroni and bologna sandwiches for Christmas.

— ADELINE

I would serve: (1) turkey, (2) stuffing, (3) sandwiches (salami or bologna), (4) deviled eggs, (5) chicken nuggets, (6) barbecued ribs.

– J.P.

I would serve Father Peter's old-fashioned Christmas dinner, with ham, fruit, and his old-fashioned green beans. I really like Father Peter's old-fashioned cooking. If you are an old Texas person, you all better hurry down to Boys Town. Come check out Father Peter's old-fashioned cooking, 'cause I tell you all what: You guys don't want to miss this feast!!

– CARISSA

CHAPTER 4

Memories

Reading *A Christmas Carol* by Charles Dickens is a good example of how to get in the Christmas spirit. Enjoying O. Henry's *Gift of the Magi* is another example. We use both of these stories at Boys Town. Although both contain distressing elements, the main characters grow and learn, and the stories' endings are uplifting.

It would be nice if all our memories could be happy and positive. Many of our boys and girls have happy memories of previous holidays, but much of our healing here at Boys Town comes from learning how to deal with bad and hurtful memories in order to clear the way for positive future holidays, without the baggage that comes from old, untreated wounds. Here are some best and worst Christmas memories:

My happiest memory of Christmas was when I was little. My sister and I would wake up and run to the tree and see all the presents. We'd get dressed and go to church with all of our family. On the way home, we'd sing songs. The day was filled with games and storytelling. Then we'd eat Christmas dinner. We'd all help clean up. Then we would sometimes go to a movie. It was fun.

— MANOLO, AGE 14

The worst Christmas that I ever experienced was my first Christmas without my mother. My heart was broken. I was nine years old without a mother. I feel sad all year round. When I was eight years old, my mom and dad gave me the best Christmas ever. All my family was there. It was like a reunion. I thank God for that memory. My mom has gone to heaven. I am now fifteen and I know that a Christmas like my eighth one will never come again until someday I grow up and have my own family to share with.

— JENNA, AGE 15

My worst Christmas was last year when I was locked up and had no one with me. This year will be my best Christmas. I have God in my heart now.

— EVAN, AGE 13

The worst Christmas I ever experienced was the year my great-grandmother passed away. She meant the world to me. She helped raise me when my parents weren't around. That Christmas I was only eight, but I still felt part of me was missing as I opened presents. Every night I pray with the rosary that was in her hand when she died. When I pray, it feels like I am holding the world in my hands. I am holding her hand and the Lord's too.

— WENDY, AGE 13

My happiest memory of Christmas was when I was ten years old. We were really poor and we didn't have many presents. We had a cardboard tree we made out of a box and wrapping paper. It was the best because we were all happy. We didn't even care that we had nothing because we had each other.

— JAIME, AGE 16

I have had a lot of bad Christmases. I haven't really ever had a family. My dad just left. He never even said goodbye when we were kids. My mom does alcohol, so I've never really had a family. That is all I've ever really wanted. My mom was always drinking. Her boyfriend was drinking. I tried to be alone on Christmas so I wouldn't have to be around the pain. I have a feeling that this Christmas at Boys Town will be my best. I feel like I have a family.

— GEORGE, AGE 13

I would have to say that I have not had a "worst Christmas." Even when I had one that was not so good, it wasn't bad. After all, the Lord was still there and so was my mom.

— JARROD, AGE 10

The worst Christmas I ever had was when I ran away last year and went to Los Angeles with my ex-boyfriend. He said he loved me. Boy, did I learn a lesson. On Christmas Day, he said he was going to get us something to eat. That is the last I ever saw of him. That was the first time in my life that I turned to the Lord and told Him that I needed His help and would trust Him.

— BETH, AGE 16

The worst Christmas I ever spent was in the past when I did not know who God was and what Bethlehem meant. I never really knew about Christmas until I came to Boys Town.

— JEREMY, AGE 10

The best Christmas was the first Christmas with both my parents. I had just been adopted and had never experienced Christmas before with parents who wanted to show me love.

— MITCH, AGE 14

The worst and best Christmas were the same Christmas. Our house was robbed. All our presents were stolen. My mom had saved up for a long time to make Christmas special.

— CAROLYN, AGE 16

My happiest Christmas was my first Christmas at Boys Town. We had a blast because everyone was so happy and we were glad to be around each other. We made sure we thanked God. We showed great appreciation to one another. We did not complain.

— JUAN, AGE 15

My happiest Christmas was when my dad was able to buy a telescope on time for me with his own money. My dad used to buy me things with drug money. It really upset my mom. But that Christmas she was really proud of my dad for making a change.

— JOHNNY, AGE 14

I have never had a bad Christmas. We are a poor family. A poor family always has Christmas gifts of love and giving thanks. That is why I like Christmas a lot.

— MIGUEL, AGE 13

My worst Christmas was when me and my brother were taken to my dad and we didn't know where we were going. My mom woke us up at 2 a.m. and put us in the car and drove us to another town. She knocked on the door and told my dad, "Here are your kids." She said that she was leaving with her boyfriend. She never came back and I have not seen her since.

— TEA, AGE 15

The best Christmas we had was when we got evicted. We ended up spending Christmas in a motel. We didn't have much but what made it such a good Christmas was that my mom and my brother and I were all together, safe from harm for a while anyway.

— PAM, AGE 13

My best Christmas is probably going to be this one because now I have love in my heart and I know I don't have to give material gifts to family and friends so they will like me. I can give my love to them.

— JASON, AGE 16

Any Christmas is bad that has no love in it. That is why my Christmases have all been good because they have had lots of love.

— ROLLIE, AGE 14

My happiest memory was my first Christmas at Boys Town. I am so used to fighting, yelling, and crying when I spent Christmas with my family. But at Boys Town it was pleasant, warm, loving, and I was truly happy. It was my first peaceful Christmas.

— BARB, AGE 16

The year I was five, my grandmother passed away. After her death, Christmas was no longer the same. Yet when she was alive she always told me to believe in Christmas. She always told me Christmas is something no one could ever take from me. She had a way of letting me know she believed in me. She always said that money wasn't what made Christmas, but family did. My grandmother was right. We all need to believe in Christmas.

— BENJAMIN, AGE 13

The thing that hurt me the most about Christmas was that I wasn't able to spend it with my father, who left me nine years ago. It just didn't feel the same without him. It was so good when I was able to run up to him and hug him for the things he got me. He left us. He made Christmas worth having.

— TINA, AGE 14

My happiest memory of Christmas was when my family got together at my aunt's house. We had fun. We were happy. We cooked a large dinner. We gave and received gifts. We laughed at jokes and we were serious at times, but we never argued. We showed the togetherness that every family should have.

— JACK, AGE 15

In past Christmases, I was hurting my family by doing drugs and alcohol and cutting school. My mother would talk to me, but I would not listen. It was bad enough that she was a single parent raising two young kids, working and paying a mortgage and buying us clothes and shoes, and there I was robbing and stealing and bringing home dirty money. I was angry.

— KYLE, AGE 17

The best Christmas I ever had was when I was little. My family was together. They were never gone. My brothers would be there and my mom and dad and we would all be together. We would sing songs and make jokes.

— KRISTIN, AGE 13

The best Christmas I have experienced was my first Christmas at Boys Town. I remember being so upset and our Assistant Family-Teacher said something that changed my world around. She told me why would I dwell on the fact that I can't go home when all of these people at Boys Town are here for me now.

— BRIANNA, AGE 14

One Christmas I took off with my friends and used drugs the entire day. I left my parents behind and hurt myself. I know now how much I hurt my parents.

— KURT, AGE 16

My best Christmas was when I was with the people I love most. My mom and dad and grandparents. It was better than any gift bought with money.

— MICHAEL, AGE 13

My happiest Christmas was this: I always wanted a red wagon, but I thought they were for rich kids until my dad came home with a red wagon for me and he let me have it on Christmas Eve instead of waiting.

— REGINA, AGE 13

I am praying that this will be my best Christmas. I can feel the love around me and it brings tears to my eyes. So many people love me and I have never realized. I know now they really do care and so do I.

— LINDSAY, AGE 17

I will try to make this Christmas my best ever. I will try to get close to the Lord. I will kneel at the crib. I will give Jesus my heart.

— GIGI, AGE 8

CHAPTER 5

Letters to Santa

The children of Boys Town's Wegner Middle School have no trouble generating enthusiasm for the Christmas holiday preparations. Important to those preparations are the annual letters to Santa Claus.

Dear Santa,

I've heard that Rudolph has been getting a little tired. Maybe he needs a break. I would like a nice train for Christmas. I hope I'm not asking too much of you. But I have been a really good boy. So I think I deserve something like that. I know you know my good buddy Father Peter. If you could drop the train off at his house, I'm sure he wouldn't mind getting it to me. Thank you, Santa.

— SIGNED, CHRIS

Dear Santa,

I have always wanted a Barbie doll. I also would like a friendship necklace so I can give it to my aunt because she is a good aunt. She took care of me when my mom and dad died. So I want to pay her back in a good way by giving her a friendship necklace.

— SARA

Dear Santa,

How is Mrs. Claus getting along? I hope she is doing good. I don't want as much as I did last year. I only want a watch that has Mickey Mouse on it. See, I don't want that much stuff. Christmas is gonna be great, and I hope you get everywhere.

— YOUR FRIEND, NICOLE

Dear Santa,

This Christmas I would like a skateboard. I've been a very good little angel. How is the Mrs? I hope the reindeer are doing fine. One more thing, could I please have a black cat? Thank you very much. Bye.

—Your sweet little angel, Julius

Dear Santa,

How is it at the North Pole? How is Rudolph? Is his nose still blinking? Is he getting enough food? Are you coming this Christmas? I wonder if you can fit down our chimney. This Christmas do you think I could get a Super Nintendo, skateboard and skates?

— YOUR FRIEND, ENRIQUE

P.S. Please try to lose weight.

Dear Santa,

I have been good. I don't want much for Christmas. All I want is what you think I should have. Do you have any new reindeer this year?

— JESSE

Dear Santa,

You are a jolly fellow. I see you have lost weight. Good! You needed to. I have been a good boy this year. I hope your reindeer are doing well. Are you ready to hear what I would like from you, Santa? I would like a little time with my parents. Thank you, Santa, for all the love you have given and the happiness and the gifts.

— SINCERELY, PAUL

Dear Santa,

For the first time in my life I want for Christmas a good education so I can do something with my life when I get older and do good in college. All kids have dreams. This is my dream. Thanks.

— LAVELL

CHAPTER 6

Don't Let the Grinch Steal Christmas

Did you ever notice that your worst trip to the dentist and your best vacation were both a disappointment? The expectations about your vacation were too high. And the expectations about your trip to the dentist were too low.

There is a lesson here that will help you keep the Grinch away from your home during the holidays.

Everybody thinks Christmas is supposed to be a time of great joy, not a time of unhappiness.

We expect feelings of togetherness. Yet we sometimes feel lonely. We have feelings of wanting to give as much as we can. Yet feelings of frustration arise because there isn't enough money.

These feelings of loneliness and frustration and unhappiness affect our thinking. Little fears set in: "The big Christmas dinner at Grandma's is going to be terrible." "This Christmas is going to be as bad if not worse than last."

That negative thinking triggers more negative feelings. And then, along with your negative thoughts and feelings, you also realize your behavior must be positive at these "dreadful events." They will all seem so hypocritical, so empty, and so phony.

You can't hide too much what you feel inside from your kids. When the Grinch is already at the door, how do you tell him, "Go away. Nobody's home."

The answer is to do two things right away. First, start changing your thinking. You really can make this season a better one:

- Yes, you will be going to events that you may not enjoy. But they are not going to be terrible. You can use good, positive humor (not sarcasm) to lighten them. Keep your attendance at these events short whenever possible. And if your adolescents accompany you, tell them how much you, as their mother or father, appreciate their going. Talk about it with them; laugh with them. Then look forward to a little fun with your children afterwards.

- "You can really help your mom by going to this event and using your good skills." "I know it is hard for you, but I appreciate your doing it." Use positive rather than negative statements: "Impress on these folks our best family skills." It really works.

- Be sure that husband and wife are talking to each other early and often. Don't let potentially troublesome events come as a surprise.

Second, change your behavior. Have you ever noticed the tendency not to utilize good social skills at the holiday season? At other times of the year we compliment people more. But because we're feeling bad, we skip it now. Have you ever noticed that at other times of the year we enjoy praying and get a lot of satisfaction from it? Yet we skip the behavior at Christmas.

Did you ever notice that we think of Christmas as a day instead of a season? Christmas really starts the first day of Advent, slowly builds, and goes all the way to the Feast of the Three Kings. If one or two or three of those days aren't so good, who cares? We can make the others good. If we mess up on Christmas, we can make the next day better.

Use your social skills. Have everybody in your family do so. That includes giving compliments, receiving compliments, having good peer relations, and sharing with your spouse positively.

I know of one family with very small children. During the first week of Advent, they put out their Christmas nativity scene. They ask each of their children to put one piece of straw in the manger "for Baby Jesus" every time they do an act of kindness for someone during the season. Using social skills in this way is putting our faith into action.

The three key elements here are thoughts, feelings, and actions. By moving our thoughts into the positive zone and by doing the same with our behaviors, we will surprise ourselves at how some of our feelings move in the same direction, too.

Boys Town students have had Christmases in their lives when the Grinch was present. But they have had the chance to reflect on those times and then move on to healing. Now they can turn things around and offer a gift of love to someone else.

Once there was a Christmas when the Grinch stole my spirit. All I wanted was to take. I did not want to give. I wanted to take, take, take instead of give, give, give. I did not want to give to anyone but when they gave all they could to me, all I said was "thanks." I did not care how they felt. I just wanted to open, open, open.

Now I look back at that Christmas and say, why would I do a thing like that? Now what I try to do is give more than I receive and that makes me feel a lot better.

— LAILA, AGE 11

The Grinch who stole my Christmas was my real mom. She was the kind of person who should never have had any kids. She didn't know how to treat us. She abandoned us. Every Christmas she would be running around and not be with us. I never knew where my real mom would be.

The gift of love I would like to give this season would be the gift my adopted mom gave me. She adopted me and my sister. When bad things happened in my family, we would always go over to her house for Christmas and she made it so much fun.

She had four children of her own but she always loved us as much as she loved her own children, no matter what the case was. She never gave up on me, either.

I love my adopted mom so very much.

— BILL, AGE 13

Once a long time ago a Grinch stole my Christmas. She was never a Grinch until that Christmas. It all started off with a bad morning. My sister was very upset. She did not get very much sleep all night. She got into an argument that morning with everyone who said or tried to do anything with her or for her. When we would play games she would sit. She refused to take part. When Christmas dinner came, she would not eat and said, "I hate this food." She did not have to say that. We all knew she was in a bad mood.

But we put it behind us and we went to the presents and to our traditional reading of the Bible. She did not do the readings with us. She did open her presents with us, however. When someone asked to see what she got, she would growl like a dog in a fight with life. She was fine the next day. We were all mad at her but we got over it.

— JACKIE, AGE 15

CHAPTER 7

Christmas Meditation

Every year we ask people across America to write a few words of Christmas encouragement to our Boys Town children. Thousands of cards pour in.

We take them over to our Wegner School. We put them on a counter where even the smallest child can reach them…big mounds of them. We say, starting the Monday after Thanksgiving, "As you go from one class to another, grab a card and read it. People across America are sending you encouragement and love. God's Christmas message is here for you to take hold of: 'Today you will know that the Lord comes. At daybreak, you will see His glory.'"

It is so important for my children and for you as well to let the light that comes from Bethlehem save all of us from the danger of accepting the darkness of our lives and of our world.

I want my children to read John 3: 19-20: "Light has come into the world. People love the darkness rather than the light because their deeds were evil. For everyone that does evil hates the light, neither comes to the light lest his deeds should be reproved."

That is why we so desperately need to celebrate Christmas. Those who celebrate Christmas accept their own insufficiency. They are much more inclined to fault themselves than others. They know they are flawed. They know that they are very much in need of redemption. They need the light of Christmas as a source of strength to renew their own lives and to help free children and those who live in darkness and the shadow of death.

"Do not be afraid for behold I bring you good news of great joy. To you is born this day in the city of David a savior who is Christ the Lord." (Luke 2: 10-11)

Christmas has year after year cheered up my own Boys Town kids who "sit in darkness and the shadow of death." Christmas provides strength for those who struggle against the ravages of abandonment and abuse. Christmas can cheer and provide strength for you, too. No wonder it is the season of hope. What should we do to gain access to this strength and hope?

Start by reading the scriptures. You will find them in any church during this season. Read them slowly as a way to begin.

Then you also need to read the Christmas hymns. Take one or two lines that you like and reflect on them for a day or two.

Go out of your way to do something kind for someone else:

- A little cheering up of someone in your family.

- A little extra attention and love.

- A little extra energy.

Now comes the important moment. Go to a church. Kneel before the manger. Give the Lord the Christmas gift that He wants – your anger, your troubles, your sins. Don't take them back. Let Him have them; that is what He wants from you for Christmas. In exchange, He will give you joy.

CHAPTER 8

Gifts of Healing

The most important gift many Boys Town youth receive is not found beneath a decorated tree. Rather, the gift that is a priceless treasure comes from a chance for hope and healing.

The gift that could most help my healing this Christmas would be for me to learn to forgive my family and my family to learn to forgive me for what I did to them.

— TONYA, AGE 16

I would like to think about other people instead of myself. Most of the time I put myself first in line. I know that this is not helpful. I want people to like me for who I am and not judging me by the way I look. My main wish is to get along better with my dad. I just want to show him how much I love him.

— STACY, AGE 13

The gift that could most help my healing at Christmas would be for my family to get together, to gather around the tree, to open Christmas presents – and really mean it with a good heart and to laugh and be happy as a real family.

— LISA, AGE 13

The gift that could most help my healing at Christmas would be for my mom to notice that I am starting to change for the better.

— MARY, AGE 13

The gift that could help my healing this Christmas would be if my mother and father would get along. As a teenager, I tried to get my mother and father back together. At seven years old, I was forced to make the decision where I wanted to live – with my mom or my dad. I just wish I would have never had to make that decision. I love both of them. I hope that at least at Christmas they will be kind to each other.

— TOMMY, AGE 14

The gift that could start a little healing in my life is the gift of every prayer that someone says for me and my family. A prayer is something pure and something special for me. I believe that without prayer, no one is happy in this world. I'm also asking for the gift of being strong toward the things that are harmful for my life.

— MARILYN, AGE 17

I need to stop lying to myself and to the people I love. I need to stop blaming other people for my mistakes. I need to start admitting my own mistakes and work through them, not by myself but with the help of people I love. So the gift I would like is a little honesty this Christmas. Honesty with myself to begin with.

— JED, AGE 16

*The gift that could most help my
healing this Christmas would be that I
could find God in my life and that He
would help me know the real meaning
of Christmas. It is not about the most
presents that you can get. It is about
opening your heart to receive God's
love, being with your family, and
having a joyful Christmas.*

— JOE, AGE 17

I thought Christmas was supposed to be happy. Not at our house. The thing that would help my family heal is to get along and listen to what Jesus has to say.

— TORIN, AGE 13

The best gifts that could heal me this Christmas would be to meet my real father and to know that he is proud of me and loves me. I have always felt that there was part of me missing. I want the memories of someone who is overprotective, plays catch with me, and is always there reading the newspaper in the morning, and saying good morning and smiling. I don't think I will ever meet my real father, but my Family-Teacher is pretty close.

— AMY, AGE 13

What I would really like to see happen this Christmas is that everyone would be having a fun time and just sit around and open presents and talk in peace. I would love to see all the homeless get a chance to celebrate Christmas. I would like to see the news where no one dies on Christmas Day and that everyone got along.

— FRANK, AGE 13

The gift that could start a little healing in my family this Christmas would be forgiveness and acceptance. I know what I have done and I am willing to change. I hope my family will be willing to forgive me and accept that forgiveness and put the past in the past.

— BOB, AGE 15

The gift that could start a little healing in my family would be for me to give back what has been given to me. Boys Town has given me the opportunity to set my priorities. I don't mind giving up things to get better things and I think the best gift I received was the chance to come to Boys Town and work on my joys.

— RAY, AGE 15

CHAPTER 9

A Season, Not a Day

I am the proud father of more than 500 boys and girls here at Boys Town. And as a father, one of the things I had to learn was how to make Christmas happy for children burdened with industrial strength troubles: abandonment, neglect, abuse.

Christmas is a time for family. How could my children be happy if so many of their families were toxic, terrible, and tragic?

It's one of the great lessons I've learned in life, and I'd like to share some steps to help you make the Christmas spirit come alive in your home:

1. Get a grip on holiday anxiety.

At the root of much of the uneasiness about the holiday season is something called anxiety. It's pretty easy to understand. There are two components to anxiety.

The first component is unpredictability. We get anxious over the holiday season because we hear two messages. The one message is, "'Tis the season to be jolly." And the other message is, "You don't know when you get up on Christmas Day if it will be happy or hectic – a day made in heaven or a day made somewhere else." You can't predict that.

The second factor is a feeling of loss of control. You really feel anxiety if, on top of your inability to predict what kind of a day it will be, you won't be able to control it even if it is bad. In other words, you won't be able to make it better. So there is coming up a 24-hour period called Christmas, and you don't know if it's going to be good or bad, and you can't control the outcome. And, of course, it's supposed to be wonderful, marvelous, terrific.

2. Make Christmas a season, not a day.

If you make Christmas a season, then you have four or five weeks to create happy events. And with just a little good effort and prayer, you have a very good chance of creating quite a few happy events in those four or five weeks from the First Sunday of Advent to New Year's Day.

For one thing, you won't discount the events before Christmas: "They don't count. The only thing that counts is Christmas Day." If you have four or five weeks, you'll allow yourself a bad day or two due to weather or work or sickness or just plain grumpiness.

Christmas parties start early in December. (It may not seem correct, but they do.) Take advantage of them. The Lord will bless you for it.

Get into the Christmas season by decorating. Some like to do it slowly, and some like to do it all at once. Either way, you need to do it and not wait until the last day when anxiety starts to build.

On the Sundays of Advent, have some festive dinners. They don't have to be elaborate. You can have festive wieners and beans! Give yourself and your children permission to have secret Santas.

Do service for God or others, too, but do it without anxiety. For example, decide that you are going to fast for half a day or a day. But don't decide when until you get up in the morning. Someday when you get up in the morning and feel terrific and feel like fasting, then do it that day. Donate the money you would have spent on food to a local shelter or other charitable cause. Surprise yourself. Surprise your kids.

Have days for making cookies. But don't decide what day until the day before. It reduces anxiety and increases the fun.

Christmas is a season, not just a day.

3. Make Christmas Day happy.

Well, the great day has arrived. When you get up on Christmas morning, say to yourself, "I am going to make this a good day because the Lord Jesus has been born into my life." Try to get to church a little early. There is less anxiety and more recollection that way.

When it comes time for the Christmas dinner, make it a big deal. By that I mean, insist that everyone be in a good mood. I mean insist. If someone is crabby, banish that person to the outer darkness and tell him or her to come back as soon as disposition improves.

For this to work, you need to enlist at least one other member of your family as a co-conspirator to make Christmas a happy day.

Make sure your kids say thank-you for their gifts. You may have to prompt them. That's good, too.

Whatever you do, put a smile on your face and a happy thought in your mind. The results will be happy feelings galore before the end of the day.

4. Make the days after Christmas very special.

In times past, the twelve days of Christmas were a marvelous tradition. You don't have to have twelve days; you can have two or three, and they don't even have to be in a row.

If you like shopping, get up early the day after Christmas for all the bargains. If you don't like shopping, sleep in the day after Christmas while all those other crazy people go after the bargains.

If you really want to have a lot of fun, save a little money for presents after Christmas. They are much cheaper.

Be sure you get to church one day during Christmas week. Then listen to the readings. There will be a message there for you from the good Lord, born at Bethlehem.

These are the days the Lord has made. Let us be glad and rejoice in them.

CHAPTER 10

How Santa Met Mrs. Claus

Children have a delightful gift for creativity and imagination. We asked Boys Town students to put that creativity to work in imagining the meeting of Mr. and Mrs. Santa Claus.

A long, long time ago, on a cold, dark night, Santa was walking down the street. He was about 23. He was walking home from the 7-Eleven.

Santa always felt alone and afraid and that was his special place for him to go. He wasn't alone because he didn't have any friends. He was alone because he was afraid to let people into his heart. He was always afraid of someone hurting his feelings. It was as cold as ice outside. And he couldn't wait to get the feeling of warmth from his own home.

Then, out of nowhere, he heard a sad cry, like an angel who lost its way home. He walked over to where he heard the cry. He saw a young woman about his own age crying. Santa Claus had heard cries like that before. It reminded him so much of himself. "Why are you crying?" Santa asked with great concern. She said, "It seems that no one cares anymore about anything. I have no friends at all. My parents don't even care."

The young woman cried on and on. Santa replied, "I'll be your special friend. Maybe if we both work together we could get everyone to be more happy with what they have and who they have."

Just then an angel appeared to them and said, "God has chosen you to spread the news of Jesus Christ being born. Make it a lot of fun. Make it full of joy." The angel disappeared and the world began to change.

They both saw a whole bunch of reindeer, a toy factory, a cozy house, and a sled. From there on, Santa filled the young woman's heart with joy and he spread the joy to everyone and the young woman became Mrs. Claus. Neither of them was ever alone again. Merry Christmas.

— SIMONE

Santa met Mrs. Claus at McDonald's one day. She was chatting with Father Peter when Santa walked in and Father Peter introduced them.

Santa took her to give presents to all the kids. They fell in love and later Father Peter married them at Dowd Chapel. They became Family-Teachers and had a set of little Santas.

— SEAN

Once upon a time there was a man named Nick Claus. Nick liked to explore the world. Nick does not know where he is from and he knows nothing about his family. Nick loves kids and helping people. He always shared and made sure that everyone around him was happy also.

One day Nick was exploring Greenland. He noticed a boat sinking, and people yelling for help. So he grabbed three life jackets, jumped in and swam out to help. He grabbed the closest two people and gave them the other jackets and he brought them to shore. The next day he got up and checked on the people he saved. One was a lady 21 years old named Holly

Joy. Holly was so happy to be alive and they became friends.

Walking around Greenland they met some elves that owned a toy store and Nick and Holly and the elves became close friends.

The next day they decided to go as far north as possible. One of the elves wanted to but the only problem was that if he went, all 75 elves had to go too.

As they went north, they came upon a herd of reindeer, about 30 of them. One even had a red nose. They were attended by a snowman who said that Santa and Holly could have them for free. And it was good that some of them could fly. Well, that's how Santa got the idea: "I believe that we could use a real big sled and between 8 and 10 of the reindeer that could fly to pull the sled through the air and we could give away toys. Let's try it on the night of December 24th."

On the day of December 24th, Nick asked Holly to marry him. She accepted and on the morning after handing out the toys, they had a big wedding. They became the Clauses. Please remember on the night before the wedding they will drop off presents to all the good kids. Have a Merry Christmas.

— Derek

Actually, I just happen to know first-hand how Santa met his wife. I'll tell you as long as you promise not to tell anyone.

One morning Santa went to the Elf Agency because he needed a few more elves for work. Business was going to be especially busy. As you know, everyone goes to the Elf Agency because we all need them.

"What are you doing here in Elf Agency?"

"Getting an elf, what else?"

"You look hungry. What is your name?"

"My name is Santa Claus."

"That's a strange name, but you look nice."

"Would you like to go out for lunch?" said Santa.

"Yes, if you will wait for me for 15 minutes."

Later on, they got married and had children and have lived at the North Pole ever since. You might want to know how I know this. Well, I fixed it all up. My name is Cupid Delaney and I'm the one who makes people fall in love with each other. But please remember: You promised not to tell – it's my secret.

– COLLETTE

Make a Christmas to Remember

[This originally appeared as a message from Father Peter to Boys Town students as they were preparing to go on home visits for Christmas break.]

> "The world has three
> kinds of people:
>
> Those who make Christmas happen,
>
> Those who watch it happen, and
>
> Those who don't know
> what hit them."

In the coming holiday season, let's all move beyond watching. Here are some suggestions that will help each of you to make Christmas happen as a happy and joyful season:

1. Make a list.

Sit down and divide a sheet of paper into two columns. In one column, put down one or two or three Christmases that you remember as being very unhappy. Bad things happened. In the other column, list one or two or three Christmases that you remember as being very warm and joyous. Good things happened.

Now ask yourself why the bad Christmases were so unhappy. The answer is plain:

- God was left out.

- Drugs and alcohol were in.

- Fighting and bitterness were in.

- People were hurting each other sexually.

Then ask yourself why the joyous Christmases were so happy:

- God was at the center of the celebration.

- Drugs and alcohol were absent.

- Kindness replaced fighting and goodness replaced hurting people.

- Someone made good things happen.

So you know what you have to do to make Christmas very happy this year. You can make good things happen.

2. Make a list, and check it twice.

Write down on your sheet of paper on the side of a happy Christmas the names of one or two people you want to keep very close to during this Christmas season. This is a good start on making Christmas happen.

You don't want to spend a lot of time with grumpy people or druggies or hang out with your old friends who always got you into trouble. You want to make sure you spend some time every day with a person who is a good, positive role model for you. Perhaps it's a grandma. Perhaps it's an aunt or uncle. Perhaps it's your big brother or big sister.

Show them this sheet of paper, and talk to them about it.

3. Tell the Lord your plans about how you are going to make Christmas happy and joyous this year.

Share with God in prayer what you have written. Put your vacation in His hands.

I pray that each and every one of you will have the most happy Christmas you have ever experienced. God bless you now and always.

CHAPTER 12

Church on Christmas Day

There is one desire which we all have at the beginning of life and which we also cherish at the end of life. When we come into this world from the hand of God, we want to be held. More than anything else, we want human warmth. We do not want to be lonely.

When we leave this life and return into the hands of God, we want one thing more than anything else: We want to be held. We do not want to be lonely. More than anything else, we need human warmth.

As we begin to grow to ages one, two, three, four, and five, we want to believe in the beauty of life:

- in its vibrancy
- in its fun
- in its joy

We want to be surrounded by the energy of life.

During these years we want to turn away from the ugliness of life:

- the boredom
- the pain
- the sorrow

We want to celebrate the gifts of the Christmas season:

- Christmas lights, not darkness
- Christmas warmth, not cold
- Christmas togetherness, not loneliness
- Christmas enthusiasm, not unhappiness

As we grow up and move beyond those young years, we may not believe in Christmas as much as before:

- We experience a loss.
- We think growing up means putting up lights, but not getting excited.
- We express Christmas warmth, but don't feel it.
- We feel lonely, even when physically with others.
- We feel helpless to stop this process.
- We are, indeed, helpless unless we get in touch with the Spirit of Christmas.

As children, Christmas dinner is exciting. It is tasty and nutritious, and it is fun to be together. Children are easily hurt when the dinner is neither tasty nor fun.

As we grow older, we don't celebrate Christmas dinner as much as before. We think that growing up means making nice food, but not really opening our hearts to joy. We feel helpless to stop this unless we get in touch with the Spirit of Christmas.

As little children, we loved the Lord. How we marveled at the story of Bethlehem! How we knelt at the manger! How we gave Baby Jesus our hearts! We set that all aside when we believed less in Christmas and when we started eating in sadness.

What does all of this have to do with church and Christmas this year? Go to church. Take a look at the manger scene. There is a present there – one present only – for you and everyone in church. Let the Babe of Bethlehem back into your life. Welcome Him enthusiastically. Make sure your Christmas dinner is tasty and fun.

> *Go tell it on the mountain*
> *Over the hills and everywhere*
> *Go tell it on the mountain*
> *That Jesus Christ is born.*

CHAPTER 13

Santa's Most Unusual Christmas

In the imaginations of our Wegner Middle School students, Santa has had to overcome some pretty amazing obstacles to deliver gifts on Christmas Eve. It's a good thing he has 364 days each year to recover!

On Christmas Eve, Santa was flying in his sleigh when he was approached by a UFO which sucked Santa and his sleigh like a hot air balloon inside their spacecraft.

Santa thought the inside looked like a pile of computer parts. He was worried he wouldn't finish his rounds. But he had an idea. He asked the aliens what they would like for Christmas. They told Santa and he got them each what they wanted. And they let him go and Christmas was saved.

— DENNIS

Santa lost a lot of weight when he worked out during the summer. He could go and walk around all the different stores and malls in the summer to see what on earth they were selling. No one recognized him because he was so thin.

— PHIL

Santa is like an angel in the sky. He never gives up on kids. He's always there when you need him. Lots of kids need him and that's why little kids think he's real. I still think he's real sometimes, too.

— MARILEE

On Christmas Eve, Santa was on his way to the USA and crashed into the moon. How did Santa think he would get the gifts to the children of the world? One of his reindeer, Comet, said, "I have an idea. Why don't we throw the presents down to earth?"

But the presents didn't get to earth. They simply floated in space. And Santa and the reindeer did, too. Now Christmas is doomed forever.

— DOUG

Long ago back in 1876, an old man named Santa lived at the North Pole.

One day, Santa was out shopping and he saw this little girl in a dark alley all by herself. She was crying. Santa could not stand to see her cry, so he went to talk to her. She was very scared and very hurt. And Santa decided to help her.

Santa let the little girl ride with him to deliver all of the presents. They were very happy together. God bless Santa for his good work and his big heart.

— ANNA

Santa is as fat as the nutty professor. He wears a red and white costume. He is as old as my grandma. He is as kind as me. He is as smart as a teacher.

— IVAN

Remember: If you ever catch Santa in your fridge, it's a compliment.

— AMBER

On the day before Christmas, Santa said, "I want somebody new to guide my sleigh. Rudolph's nose is getting dim."

But the reindeer wouldn't let him do that. So they quit. A couple minutes later, Santa gave the reindeer an apology and let Rudolph guide his sleigh.

You could see tears in Santa's eyes that he was sad he had been inappropriate and happy he made an apology.

— MAL

Santa's sleigh was wrecked so he decided to get on a plane and drop all the presents out the window. TWA flight 2001 after two hours had engine trouble. Santa crashed in the lake. He took his bag and went on foot.

He found a cab but the cab driver got mad when he found out it was Santa because Santa had not gotten him a horse when the cab driver was little.

Santa never got to finishing all the presents and so all the kids were mad and they stopped believing in him for a while. Now you know the story of Santa's worst Christmas.

— JAKE

Once upon a time, Santa got very fat. He could not fit in his suit. Santa knew all this extra weight was going to be a real problem for his reindeer. He began to lose weight by running the stairs and lifting weights. He ate bananas, apples, pears and pineapple. He fast-walked to see in the windows who was naughty or nice.

By Christmas Eve, he had lost enough weight that he could fit in his suit and all the children had a Merry Christmas.

— SHAREE

Let me introduce myself. I am one of Santa's helpers. I have been on the job for a while. I really enjoy making toys for the little ones.

One of my fellow workers left a car on the floor. It dropped out of the bag we had for Santa. Santa came to watch and slipped on the car. He fell with a loud kerplunk. He didn't move. He was out cold.

We all looked at each other in disbelief. Mrs. Claus said that we needed to get him to his bed. We all looked at each other in utter disbelief. How could we ever lift this huge man? It took about twelve elves to carry him to his room. It took all the energy we *had. Mrs. Claus said he just might have a concussion. We would have to wait and see.*

We took turns sitting by his bedside. We were all worried sick. No one thought of resuming work or preparing for Christmas. With Santa out cold, the magic just wasn't there. Maybe there wouldn't be a Christmas this year. We would have to wait and see.

— RENESHA

CHAPTER 14

A Giving Heart

Children like to receive gifts at Christmas, but they also get great joy from giving to others. Boys Town students reflect on gifts that they'd like to share with special people in their lives.

I would choose friendship because friendship is free. I can give friendship to just about anybody that wants to be my friend. It is like hanging out and having a positive conversation. We can just go swimming, go to the park, go to the store, make different kinds of things, and go walk around town. I see friendship as a really important gift. If I give this to others who do not have friends, they will feel real good. When I do nice things for my friends, I feel real happy.

— HELEN

If I could give any Christmas gift whatsoever, I would give the gift of time to my mom. I will spend time with my mom doing the things that she likes to do this Christmas and not just what I like to do. I will clean the house for her. I will show her that I love her by being patient and appreciating who she is and what she has done for me, even when she is so very ill. I will thank her.

— BECCA

The first gift I would want to give without wrapping it up is to take a friend out to eat. The second is inviting someone over to your house on Christmas Day. The third is to give someone a hug if they are feeling bad about something. The fourth is to do someone's chore for them if they are busy with something. The fifth is to thank people that helped out on Christmas. I like these good deeds because they make people feel good when you do something for someone or get them something if they need it. I know I would like that if someone did that for me on Christmas.

— DAWN

If I could give any Christmas gift, I would give my dad the gift of going to God with his everyday problems instead of going to his beer. My dad looks for solutions to his problems in a bottle. I hope and pray this Christmas that my dad wakes up and sees what he is doing to himself and to my mom and my two sisters. I hope that he chooses the road to getting better.

— DANIEL

All the gifts that I would give are from my heart after digging beyond my selfishness. Christmas to me now is realizing what I can do for others, not what others can do for me.

— CARLA

My first gift that I would give to my mom is the gift of love and care. I have always loved my mom, but I have not been there to take care of her when she was sick. I have only taken care of my mom once when she was sick. That was when I brought her a bowl of soup when I was seven years old before I came to Boys Town.

— MARCO

Hugs are nice to give and to receive from most people. They make me feel warm inside. They are also a gift that you can give a lot. It is a great fast gift and you never run out. One time when I was feeling really bad, I gave my Family-Teachers a hug.

— JACOB

The next person who is going to receive something from me is my dad even though he is dead. I am going to try and forgive him for the things that he put me and my family through. This year's Christmas has made me realize how I need to do this.

— CHARLEY

Christmas is the time of year that you should not just be happy for the presents you receive. If you give love and not hate, you will be happy that you are being loved back instead of hated back.

— ROSS

The gift I would give is the gift of bravery. It is a hard gift to give. It means that you will have to step up to the plate and accept the challenge. It means that you have to show the world what you are made of. Bravery also means accepting decisions here at Boys Town. This is the gift of bravery.

— ZAK

I would give the gift of wisdom. Wisdom is like peanut butter on toast. Wisdom means a whole lot to people because they want to know everything in the past and future. I would also like to give love because love is like a basket of gold. It is important to me because I always wanted to have love back from my parents. I will give it at Christmas.

— Jamar

I am going to love the reaction on my brother's face when he gets the wonderful gift of sacrifice. What will help me give this to him is by spending some time with him and not leaving him to go out with friends and making him feel like he is not wanted.

— TONY

My gift of love will be a Christmas card for my sister. I will tell her I still love her and I think of her all the time. I will tell her no matter what happens we will be together, now and forever in heaven. When all the pain is over and all the tears have dried up, I can hold her in my arms and say how much I love her.

For you see, my sister is mentally retarded from birth. She always has been slow and it takes her awhile to catch on to things. Sometimes I wonder if she would even remember me if I saw her. Even though she is older than me she has always been my little sister. I am constantly thinking about her and praying that she remembers me and knows I will always love her.

Even though a Christmas card isn't much I will be able to tell her I miss her. I will put the return address on the envelope so she can write back to me.

This Christmas, pray for all the little ones around you and thank God you can see them smile. Thank God you can hug them and see the beam of light in their eyes as they open their gifts. You can never give enough thanks to God for family and friends, and most of all, life.

— LILA

You can sing a pretty song as sweet as a puppy. You can make someone's day brighter. Sometimes if you can do something for someone, then they will want to do something for you. It can make someone feel nice and positive about themselves. You just have to let them know that you care.

— SYLVIA

The first gift that I would give is to my real dad. I would give him the gift of forgiveness. This gift is harder to give than to give a million dollars. I would give him this because I think that it would give him the chance to be a better person. The second gift that I would give is to my step-dad. I would give him the gift of acceptance. Why? Because I have always denied him the right to acceptance. I think if I give him the chance to prove himself a good father, he will love me and treat me more like a daughter.

— MEGAN

*One of my five gifts of love would
be to tell others about Jesus and show
them how he works his miracles in my
life and theirs. I would also be kind
and generous to others. First of all,
cheer them up if they were in the
dumps. Then I would play a game with
them. Then I would be friends with the
person even if they don't have many
friends. After that, I would be helpful,
but not too helpful.*

— CELESTE

*If I could give any Christmas gift
this year, I would give my Boys Town
family a big hug to show them how
much I care for them and how much I
appreciate them.*

— CALLIE

*If I could give any Christmas gift
whatsoever, I would give my best
friend, Martha, a mother who truly
showed her love and concern. It really
hurts me.*

— ALLISON

If I could give one gift to someone in my family, it would be my brother. I will give him the love that I have never expressed to him before. With his declining health, it has taken me a long time to accept the way he now is. The more I can show my love to him now, the more I will love him when he joins Jesus in heaven. I need to learn not to hide my feelings.

— JOANIE

If I could give any Christmas gift whatsoever, I would give the gift of Christmas to someone who does not believe. I would let them experience the gift of the Lord. I would just be with someone who doesn't have a family to make them feel loved. And I would give the Lord my heart. My heart says it all.

— MICHELLE

For Christmas I would like to take my favorite trophy that I won this year and as a gift of love take it to my brother's gravesite and show him so that he will be proud of me. I want to share this gift with him because he was so special to me. I want him to know that I love him.

— DONNY

If I were to give a gift to someone at Boys Town, it would be to my Family-Teachers. I would give them charity and the feeling that they have helped a youth like me to do better. They have been by me when I needed it. They have also given me the options and they have talked to me and helped me get better.

— BRANDON

If I could give any gift at Christmas, I would give to the Lord my word that I will never be seen inside of a prison cell again. I will start to learn more about feelings and not just hate and anger.

— ROB

I intend to give a gift to my family even though I have no money. I have love, joy, and respect that I will give to them back home.

— ROSA

My gift of love would be to make my grandma cry tears of joy. She is the most beautiful grandma in the world. When no one else cared, Grandma cared. She never stopped loving me. I remember when I was ten and we were at her house on Christmas waiting for Mom to come to open gifts. Mom came and she was drunk and made everyone unhappy and ruined our Christmas. She later apologized and I forgave her. Now she is getting help and getting better. I love my mom and hope to share this Christmas with her.

— YVONNE

*If I could give any gift to my
family back home, I would give the gift
of faith. That would be the greatest
present I could ever give. Faith in
God will bring them love and salvation.
It will also make them better people.
That gift would change their lives and
their perspective on life for the better.
And with that gift comes eternal life
and that lasts longer than any
material gifts.*

— ALEX

The gift I would give to my family this Christmas is all the love, time, laughs, and all the good memories I didn't let my family have when I was back home. Another gift would be to my mother if I can make some changes here at Boys Town. That would be the best gift I could ever give anyone. I could let her know I really do love her and I'm really sorry for all I have done and for all of the hard times I have made her go through.

— CARRIE

If I could give any Christmas gift whatsoever to the Lord, I would give the Lord me because He is the one who put me here and made Boys Town. If it weren't for God and the Boys Town He made, who knows where I would be?

— JAMIE

If I could give the Christmas spirit to someone, I would give it to my mother. I would give her a day without medication and without pain. I would give her strength and guidance to deal with her problems. I would let her enjoy Christmas.

— CONNIE

If I could give any Christmas gift whatsoever, I would give my mom, brother, and sister love and lots of hugs and kisses. And I would give them presents. They have all helped me with my problems. I want them to know I love them always.

— WILLIAM

I have a special gift to give this Christmas. I am going to my mom's house. She doesn't have a lot of money. I already got gifts for my little brothers and I bought the food for our Christmas. But I think the special gift I'm giving this Christmas is that I have changed a lot, and I am going to be with my family and have a positive attitude.

— KATIE

I got the Christmas spirit this season by giving to my family the gift of change. I think that gifts don't always have to come in gift-wrapped package form. I believe a gift is something that comes straight from the heart. I thank the Lord for giving me a second chance to do well and to succeed. I give Him me because I am one of His children. Merry Christmas.

— ADAM

If I could give any Christmas present to my family, I would give them the love they need that I never gave them in the past. And I would give to the Lord my special love. I really need to get help from the Lord for my problems, as we all do. You see, I am already catching the Christmas spirit.

— KIRSTIN

Book Credits

Editing: Lynn Holm
Production: Mary Steiner
Cover Design: Margie Brabec
Page Layout: Anne Hughes